T0197352

Cotton Balls

Florence Zimmerman

ISBN: 978-1-4669-0911-3 (sc)
ISBN: 978-1-4669-0912-0 (e)

Trafford rev. 01/24/2012

 www.trafford.com

North America & International
toll-free: 1 888 232 4444 (USA & Canada)
phone: 250 383 6864 ♦ fax: 812 355 4082

The threat of the KKK had me in a constant state of fear, even when I slept. The horses would chase me. A dark-haired boy rode on a dark horse. A blond-haired boy rode on a white horse. They chased me into the cotton fields—through the grapevines and onto the highway. I was running as fast as I could. My heart was pounding, and tears streamed down my face. Just as the blond guy reached me, I would wake up. It was only a dream.

"It's time to go," my mother said, tugging on my shoulders.

I jumped out of bed, washed my face in cold water, and donned my dress. I slipped on my shoes. I was ready.

"Be right back!" Mom called out. She picked the baby up and hastily walked out the door. I watched as she crossed the alley and went into Mrs. Hattie's bungalow. I kept peeping out the window and praying she would hurry so we wouldn't miss the bus. She finally returned without the baby. I smelled the whiskey on her breath. I backed away, turned my nose up, and exchanged that whiskey stink.

"Brother's still in bed. We're going to miss the bus."

"Oh, he's not going," she said. "He's going to stay and help Hattie with the baby. Come on—let's go." She looked down at my feet. "Where's your socks?"

"I don't know," I replied. I dropped my head.

"Oh God," she whispered, picking up the bag. Out the door and down the street we went. I took a deep breath, elated that we were still going.

The sun was shining bright. The day was cold and windy. The short-sleeved dress could not keep the chill bumps off my arms. I kept rubbing them. Mama looked down at me. "You cold?" she asked

"Oh, no!" I said quickly. "I'm okay." She smiled as if she knew I was lying. We kept walking. I could barely tolerate the cold as I trotted along beside her.

I had prayed this day would come. Each night after our daily prayer, I would say, "God, please bring my sister home."

My prayers were answered when a letter came from my aunt Kendra. After Mama finished reading the letter, she sighed, shook her head, and exclaimed, "I have to go and get that child."

My aunt Biggie had taken my sister, Louise, to Benson Town. She was supposed to return in two weeks. She was offered a job in North Carolina. She left Louise with my father and grandparents. We were on our way to get her, and nothing could make me turn back now, especially a little cold.

Down the street we went, passing little stores and bungalows, and when we reached Rose's, mama grabbed my hand. "We need to stop here," she said. I loved Rose's. The store was large and had lots of things to see, but today I did not want to stop—I was afraid we'd miss the bus—but mama insisted. It felt good inside the store; I stopped rubbing my arms. We headed down an aisle, and I picked up a Little Golden Book on the way. Midway down the aisle, we stopped. There in the middle of the store was a rack of coats with matching hats. Mama searched through the coats, and she finally pulled out a blue coat and hat. "Try this on," she whispered. She helped me into the coat and then the hat. They fit perfectly. Mama patted me on the shoulders and whispered for me to go stand by the door. She went off in a different direction.

After what seemed like an eternity, she came up to the counter with a bag of peanuts in her hand. "That'll be ten cents," the clerk said. Mama gave her the money. She handed Mama the bag. She left the store, and I followed.

As the big bus roared off from the station a short time later, I peered out the window as we passed stores, bungalows, and houses. They all disappeared as the bus pulled onto the highway.

Mama tapped me on the shoulder. "Want some peanuts?" she asked. She placed the peanuts, the Little Golden Book, and a pair of socks in my lap. Then she reached into one of our bags and pulled out a smaller bag. "I got to go to the bathroom," she said. "Put the socks on." She went to the bathroom, taking the small bag with her. She came back from the bathroom and sat down. A few minutes later, she was asleep. Every few minutes, she would lean over on me and sit back up. Finally, she whispered, "Let me get by the window." I slid past her, and she moved over to the window, laid her head against it, and fell asleep. I opened the Little Golden Book and stared at the little lamb whose fleece was white as snow. I kept thinking about how my mama did not pay for the coat, hat, socks, and the Little Golden Book.

Aunt Kendra and Uncle Tim met us at the bus station. We arrived at my grandparents' house late in the evening, just as the sun was setting. The car stopped in front of an enormous house on tall brick pillars. The lattice that surrounded the house had fallen in places. The white paint that had once covered the house had rolled up like shaved wood. "We're here," Uncle Tim said. "Old Wire Road. Everybody out."

I was still chattering when Uncle Tim opened the door and helped me out. My feet had barely touched the ground when I heard a bell. I looked up and realized that the sound was coming from a bell around a cow's neck. Each time the cow swished her tail, she shook her head and the bell rang. Behind the cow stood a black wash pot, fire blazing. As the cold wind blew, the fire leaped up toward the sky. The bright orange glow of the sun seemed to reach down to meet the flames. A very dark-skinned woman descended the steps of the porch. She had on black attire with a red apron. A red scarf was tied around her head. I was horrified. *She's a witch,* I thought. I had seen them in my brother's comic books. I froze.

"Oh Jesus," she cried as she reached the bottom of the steps. "They brought my baby home. Come to Grandma." I wanted to run but could not move. She came over, patted me on the shoulders, and hugged me. I stood still. She began chattering with the other adults, and they all walked back toward the house. The broken screen door slammed behind them.

"Psst, psst," came a sound from under the house. I turned toward the sound. I didn't see anyone. "Psst, Psst," came the sound again. "Over here." A small boy stuck his head from behind the pillar. "Come here," he whispered. I was too frightened to move. He came from behind the pillar and peeped up at the porch as if he didn't want anyone to see him. He ran out, grabbed my hand, and pulled me under the porch. "Don't be scared," he whispered. "I'll protect you."

"Is she a witch?" I asked.

"Yes," he said, "but it'll be okay. I'm Harwin. What's your name?"

"L-lillie," I stammered.

He hugged me. "You'll be my best friend," he said. "I'll always protect you." That night, Harwin slept on a quilt beside me and three other children. I kept waking up throughout the night, and each time I fell asleep, the witch would chase me. When morning came, I was exhausted.

"Wake up, wake up!" Mama yelled as she tugged at my shoulder. "We're going to get Louise."

"Where is she?" I asked.

"Your father took her home with him," she replied.

"Where's that?" I asked. "Do we have to take a bus?"

"Oh, no," she laughed, "it's right across the field in one of the old slave bungalows. Come on. Get up." I got up and stepped on Harwin.

"Ouch," he cried out.

I reached down and rubbed the spot where I had stepped. "I'm sorry."

"That's okay," he said. "It didn't hurt. Where you going?"

"To get Louise." I smiled. "Wanna come?"

"No," he said, "I'm still sleepy." He covered his head.

We walked through the sandy fields until we reached a small shack. I was amazed that it hadn't collapsed. Mama knocked on the door. Daddy opened it, and we stepped inside. There was no floor, just sand. My sister sat in an old wooden chair in front of a rusty old tin heater. There were holes on both sides. She held a bowl of popcorn. I held on to Mama's dress.

"What is this?" Mama asked.

At the sound of Mama's voice, Louise looked up and burst into tears. Mama reached down and took the bowl, throwing it across the room. She picked Louise up and walked out. Daddy followed. "Annie, Annie!" he said. "Let me explain."

Back at Grandma's, Mama asked Aunt Kendra how could she let Louise stay over there. Aunt Kendra began to sob. "There was nothing I could do," she cried. "She was being mistreated over here. They sometimes sent her to bed without supper. I wanted to help her, but I was too afraid to try."

Mama hugged her. "I know the situation," she said. "You're a good person. I do wonder how you can take living with that witch."

"Psst, psst," came the sound. I looked down. Harwin was standing by the porch, bidding with his hand for me to come with him. I descended the steps and followed him under the porch. We built a sand castle and stomped it down. "Let's go play with some dolls," he said.

"You got dolls?" I asked, surprised.

"No, we have to make them," he said, "but you can't tell nobody. When I play with dolls, they call me a faggot."

"What's that?" I asked.

"Come on," he said with a smile. I followed him out from under the porch and into the cornfield. He went from stalk to stalk. Finally, he pulled off two ears of corn. "Hold this," he said, handing me one. I took it and began to rub the silk. "That's the hair," he said. "You have to be careful—it's easy to break." He pulled a few more ears, and we made dresses. We had been playing for hours when we heard Aunt Kendra calling.

"Harwin, Harwin, where are you? Supper is ready."

Aunt Kendra and Uncle Tim was married when she was only thirteen years old. She was now twenty-five and had five children, four boys and one girl. Harwin was the fourth born. He was six years old, one year older than me.

Harwin hastily dug a hole and buried the dolls.

"Why did you do that?" I asked.

"The witch would kill us if she knew we were pulling the corn," he said. I became even more afraid of Grandma.

Once inside, Harwin sat down at the table with the other children. All the chairs were taken. I stood by Harwin, and Louise sat on the floor. The aroma of the fried chicken and collared greens made me hungry. I could barely wait to eat. Grandma fixed plates for all the children sitting at the table. When she finished, she went to the pantry and took out a bottle of syrup and two saucers. She placed two biscuits on each and poured some syrup on them. She handed one to me and one to Louise. I sat on the floor beside Louise and ate.

After we ate, Grandma sent us out to play. Harwin grabbed my hand and led me out the door and under the porch. "I saved you something." With a grin, hereached into his pocket, pulled out a chicken wing, and handed it to me. I took the wing and pulled it apart. I gave him half, and I took half. After we ate the chicken, we sat in the sand and covered our feet.

"Harwin, Harwin, it's time to come in," Aunt Kendra called out a short while later.

We kicked the sand off our feet and ran up the steps and into the house. Harwin slept on the floor beside the bed that night.

After a breakfast of grits, butter, and a glass of milk the next morning, me and Harwin ran out and under the house to play. "Wanna make some dolls?" he asked.

"Oh, no!" I exclaimed. "I'm afraid."

"Okay, we'll do something else," he said. "I know—we'll make some furniture from sticks. When we grow up, we'll be designers. We will design furniture and do hair, okay?" I smiled. We went to look for sticks.

When we returned, Mama and Daddy had come and gone. "Where did they go?" I asked Aunt Kendra.

"They went to look for a house," she said.

"Goody," I whispered to Harwin. "We're going to stay here."

"See, I told you we'll always be friends." He hugged me.

When Mommy and Daddy returned, she was smiling. "Kendra," she said, "we found a house, and you need to make Tim get you out of this hellhole."

Mama and Daddy went back to the shack that night. We stayed with Grandma. The next day, I waited for them to return. The sun was going down. It would soon be dark. Where were they? I was sitting on the steps with tears in my eyes when Harwin came out.

"What's wrong?" he asked.

"Mommy and Daddy aren't coming back. They left us."

Harwin patted me on the shoulder and went inside. He came back with a big smile. "They're coming back." He sat down beside me, still grinning. "They went to get the other children."

"How do you know?" I asked.

"Mama said so," he said.

I got up early the next morning to wait for them. I waited and waited, and finally Uncle Tim was coming down the road. We could hear the car coming from afar.

"That's them!" Harwin shouted. He grabbed my hand and pulled me from under the porch. "Come on," he said. "They're here." We stood holding hands as Mommy and Daddy got out of the car.

Daddy was carrying the baby. Mama had a bag, and my brother dragged behind. He seemed angry, as if he did not want to move. Mama handed me the bag. I peeped inside it and saw my Raggedy Ann doll. I hugged her and handed her to Harwin. He hugged her and burst into laughter.

Mommy and Daddy went inside. They talked awhile, took the baby, and left. They did not return that day; they returned late the next evening. "We're going home tonight," Mommy said. "Just get your night things; Tim will bring the rest tomorrow." I grabbed my doll, and Daddy carried my sister. Mommy carried the baby.

As we descended the steps, I looked down and saw Harwin standing by one of the pillars. I didn't want to leave him, but I was happy to leave there. When I reached the bottom of the stairs, he kissed me on the cheek. "It's not far," he said. "I'll see you, okay?"

"Okay." I smiled and ran to catch up with Mama and Daddy.

"Is it a long way?" I asked Mama.

"No, baby, it's a short walk," she replied. We walked down the road for a few minutes, around a curve and up a hill.

When we reached the top of the hill, Daddy stopped and pointed to a house at the bottom of the hill. "That's the house," he said, "our new home."

"Last one there is a rotten egg," brother shouted. He ran down the hill, and I followed, running as fast as I could. "I beat you," he said, slapping the porch. When I reached the house, I was exhausted. I sat on the steps panting. Brother went inside. He ran back out. "Come on!" he exclaimed. "You got to see this. There's three rooms and three beds."

I went inside and found all three beds made up with white sheets and striped blankets. I jumped into one of the beds, so happy. I loved our new home, we were in walking distance from Harwin, and we were back with Daddy. "Harwin's my best friend," I said to brother as I rolled over and over in the bed.

We had been living on Old Wire Road a short time when Aunt Kendra came to visit, and Harwin came with her. I ran up the hill to meet them. Me and Harwin sat on the porch laughing, and she went inside. We heard her crying. I looked at Harwin, puzzled, and we got up and went inside. Aunt Kendra was sitting at the table with her head down. "There's just too many of us there," she cried. "I'm just about to go crazy."

"That goddamn Tim!" Daddy exclaimed. "Don't worry, Kendra. I'll talk to him."

"No!" Mama said. "You let me talk to him. I don't want y'all fighting."

Uncle Tim was coming down the road in his Model T Ford.

"Here comes that goddamn fool now," Daddy said. "Damn son of a bitch."

Aunt Kendra quickly got up. "Come on, Harwin. Let's go." They went out and got into the car. Harwin waved as they left.

A few weeks went by, and I had not seen Harwin. I was sad. I begged Mama to take me to his house. "Later," she would say, but she never took me.

I was in the yard playing one day when down the hill came Aunt Kendra and Harwin. I ran to meet them. "We're moving," he whispered.

At the house, Aunt Kendra went inside. We followed. Once inside, she began clapping her hands and singing "Good News, the Chariot's Coming."

"You're moving. Thank God you're getting out of that hellhole."

"Yep." Aunt Kendra giggled. "Thanks to you, we're moving to Marvis Town."

"How far is that?" I asked Harwin.

"Long, long ways," he said sadly. "I'm going to miss you."

I cried. I was going to lose my best friend. Months passed, and I concluded that I would never see him again.

Winter came, and we all got whooping cough. Mama made medicine out of weeds and white lightning. She told us to wash our faces with our pee when we went out to potty. When she left the room, brother whispered, "If you wash your face in that piss, you're going to die." We pretended to wash our faces with the urine.

"Did you wash your faces?" Mama asked.

"Yes," we lied. She touched our faces; they were dry.

She laughed. "You gotta wash your faces when you go out."

After a while, we all stopped coughing. Mommy said it was a miracle we all survived, especially the baby.

The stress of taking care of the four of us had taken its toll on Mama. I didn't know what had happened to her. She didn't have whooping cough, but she was sick. She stayed in bed most of the day, only getting up to cook. She put the pots on the stove and went into the bedroom. We heard a loud crash. We ran into the room to find her lying on the floor facedown.

Daddy turned her over and put his hand over her face. "Oh God!" he exclaimed. "She's not breathing." He picked her up and threw her on the bed. She didn't move. He picked her up again and threw her on the bed; her eyes opened. We stood clutching each other's hands and shoulders.

"What happened?" she asked.

"You passed out," Daddy said.

She sat up in the bed.

"I'll go get Tim to take you to the doctor," Daddy said.

"Oh, no," she said. "Get me a drink and I'll be all right till morning." He went into the kitchen and came back with some white lightning in a glass. She drank it, talked awhile, and went to sleep.

Mama was still asleep when we got up the next morning. "Is she dead?" I asked my brother.

"Don't be silly," he snapped.

She awoke later that day. "Y'all eat?" she asked. She rubbed her eyes. "Where's Shug?"

"Mr. Bud came for him," brother said. "Yeah, we ate that mess he made."

She smiled and went back to sleep.

Daddy returned that day with pans of food. As we sat down to eat, Mama woke up. "Hmmm, that smells good," she whispered. "Who cooked?"

"Betty," Daddy answered. "Want some?" Betty was Mr. Bud's wife.

He got up and went into the kitchen, returning with two plates of food. After propping Mama up in bed, he placed the plate of food on a pillow. We sat on the floor beside the bed. He sat in a nearby chair, plate in hand.

"Annie," he said between chews, "we need to move closer to town. I talked to Bud today. His sister Madalyn has a house on her place. He thinks she might let us move in it. A person could die before they can get to a doctor from out here."

"We're moving, Daddy?" brother asked. We gathered around Daddy. "Where? When?"

"I dunno," he replied, "but we're getting out of here."

We were still living on Old Wire Road. The sun was shining bright, and down the dirt road came Granddaddy riding his horse. He had a big grin on his face. "Wanna ride?" he asked.

"Yeah," I said.

"Me too!" Louise cried.

After dismounting, he picked Louise up and put her on the horse, and he placed me behind her. "Hold on tight," he said.

He pulled on the ropes, saying, "Come on, Betsy." The horse followed. We giggled as the horse traveled slowly down the dirt road, and after walking awhile, he stopped the horse. "We'd better go back now," he said. "The sun is setting."

As the horse was turning around, Louise almost fell off. She began screaming, "Take me down, take me down!"

Granddaddy tried to convince her to stay on the horse, but she refused. She kept crying. He took her off the horse, took her hand, and began the walk back. He kept trying to get her back on the horse. Each time he tried, she began crying. He finally gave up. "It'll be dark before we get back," he said. I'll have to tote you." The sun was setting fast. He picked her up and began walking faster. We were almost at the bottom of the hill when we heard a bell. He began walking even faster.

Over the hill came Grandma leading the cow. Each time the cow swished her tail, she shook her head and the bell rang. Grandma stopped on the top of the hill, waved her broom, and shouted, "Willow B, Willow B!" I stared at the sun. The trees on both sides of the road and the high hill made the orange sun look as if it touched the ground. She looked as if she floated right out of the sky.

"Better hurry," Granddaddy said. "Here comes the witch. "

Grandma was a self-proclaimed witch. Grand daddy had been a Baptist preacher until Grandma burned his bible and dared him to ever enter a church again. After that, he began calling her "the witch" and so did her children. He would hide to pray. Their children called him "the coward".

She reached the bottom of the hill just as we reached the pathway to our house. He took me off the horse. "Run, run!" he called.

I grabbed Louise's hand, and we ran to the house. I heard her yelling, "Willow B[1], I better not ever catch you down here again—never!" Granddaddy jumped on his horse and hurried off. Grandma and the cow followed, broom waving, tail swishing, head shaking, bell ringing.

---

[1]   My Grandfather's name was Willie Bogan. Grandma called him Willow B.

We peered out the window as they disappeared over the hill. Brother burst into laughter. Me and Louise began to cry.

Daddy came home from Marvis Town. When Mr. Bud dropped him off, he came in and dropped a bag of turnips on the table. "Betty sent them," he said to Mommy, "and guess what. Madalyn is letting us have the house. We're moving as soon as you are ready."

"I'm ready now," Mommy said.

We jumped up and down. "We're moving!" we shouted.

A few days later, Mr. Bud came to move us. We moved into an old house on his sister's property. She was in a mental institution in Columbia. Bud, her brother, took care of her farm while she was away. It was early spring when we moved in. Daddy helped Mr. Bud prepare the land, and Mama helped Mrs. Betty in the house. When fall arrived, we picked the cotton for Mr. Bud and his sister. When their cotton was finished, we went to help Mrs. Millie, his deceased cousin's wife.

Mrs. Millie had two brothers, Ward and Todd. They were both reputed to be members of the Klan. Mr. Ward owned a hardware store downtown. He had been supporting her since Mr. Walter died. He was not married and did not have any children. He doted on Brad. Mr. Todd was married and had two children. I had never met him and Mrs. Millie hardly ever spoke of him.

It was late October, but the days were still sunny and hot. We were working in Mrs. Millie's fields when someone called out, "Annie, Annie!" I looked up, and down a row of cotton came Mrs. Millie. She wore a red striped sundress, no shoes, and a big smile.

"How you doing, Millie?" Mommy asked. She stood up and shielded her face from the sun with her hands.

"I'm just fine," Mrs. Millie said.

"How have you been making it since Walter died?" Mama asked. "I know you miss him."

"I'm doing fine." Mrs. Millie turned, pointing to a colored man raking the yard. "Look at what he left me."

"Millie," Mama laughed, "you're going to get yourself into a world of trouble."

Mrs. Millie reached down, pulled off two balls of cotton, and handed them to Mama. "No—double trouble," she giggled. "There's two of them, Lance and Tarec. My husband kept the cotton fields hot."

Lance and Tarec were the offspring of Walter and his colored lover's; they were older than his wife, Millie. They had three children with my aunts Biggie and Jean. My grandma took care of the children. She called them "those damn Marvis children."

I liked living in Marvis Town because most of our family lived there. Uncle Tim would bring the children over on Saturday while they went to town. I had my friend back. We had real dolls now. We would hide in the cotton field to play with them because Harwin had to hide.

One afternoon Mr. Bud came down the dirt road in his rickety old truck. He stopped in front of the house. "Shug," he called out. Daddy went out and leaned on the door of the truck. They chatted for a while.

When Daddy returned, Mommy asked, "What did Bud want?"

"Madalyn is being released," he said. "Bud wants me to clean up the debris from the yard and dust the house."

Mrs. Madalyn came home a few weeks later. Daddy went every day to help her. This went on for months. One day Mrs. Madalyn came racing up the dirt road. She drove right up to the porch and jumped out the car. Me and Louise were sitting on the porch. "Where is your mother?" she asked angrily.

"She's not here," I answered.

She smiled. "Where's your daddy?"

"Inside," I mumbled. I was astounded by the sudden change in her face.

"Shug!" she yelled. Daddy didn't answer. "Shug, shug!" she called again. "I know you're in there. Come on out."

Daddy came out wiping his eyes as if he'd been asleep.

"What happened to you?" she snapped.

"What you mean, what happened to me?" he asked.

"I haven't seen you in days."

"I'm not coming back," Daddy said. "Forget that shit."

She ascended the steps and entered the porch. "Am I going to see you tonight?"

"No way," Daddy said. "I just told you."

She took a swing at him. He backed up. They began to scream at each other. Frightened, we gathered around.

"If he hits her, he's going to jail," brother whispered.

"I'll see you tonight or else," she snapped. She staggered down the steps and into the yard.

"You won't see me tonight or no other night!" he hollered.

She reached for the car door, turned around, looked at Daddy, and smiled the most wicked smile. "Don't come," she chuckled, "and you'll be sorry."

"Sorry for what?" Daddy laughed.

"Sorry for what?" she repeated. "Sorry because I'll have your black ass locked up for stealing my hog."

"What damn hog?" he asked. "Go on, woman. You're as crazy as a bedbug."

"They'll be biting your black ass in jail tomorrow night!" she screamed. "You'll see. She opened the car door, got in, slammed the door, and sped off.

"Crazy-ass woman," Daddy said. He went inside and closed the door.

Mama knew about the fight before she returned home. She was at Mr. Bud's house when Madalyn stormed in threatening to have Daddy locked up for stealing her hog.

Daddy wasn't home when Mommy came back. She questioned us, wanting to know every word Mrs. Madalyn and Daddy had said. We told her everything we could remember. As soon as Daddy walked through the door, she lashed out at him. "So you stole Madalyn's hog?"

"She didn't have no damn hog," he replied.

"I know," Mama said. "Stepped in shit that time, didn't you?"

"Is you saying I had something to do with that damn woman?" he shouted. "You know for yourself she's just a crazy troublemaker." He walked out and slammed the door.

The next morning, Mama was getting ready to go with Mrs. Millie. She called Daddy. "Shug," she yelled, "wake up! So you didn't visit Madalyn last night. What do you want me to bring you in jail?" He didn't answer.

A car pulled into the driveway and honked. I got up and peeped out the window. It was Mrs. Millie. Mommy left with her. I went back to sleep. I was relieved it wasn't the law.

The sun came through the window, awakening me. I got up and woke Louise. We went out and dug up our dolls that we had buried the day before. The moisture had caused them to peel. They looked like monsters. Louise began to cry. We heard a car coming. I tried to see whose car it was, but the dust covered everything. I thought it was the law coming to get Daddy.

The car pulled into the yard; it was Mr. Bud. He got out of the car, reached through the window, and honked the horn. Daddy came from behind the house. "How you doing, Mr. Marvis?" he asked.

Tolerable Mr. Bud said, "Look, Shug, you got to move." He took off his hat and rubbed his balding head. "I talked Madalyn out of calling the law, but she wants you out. She claims you stole her hog."

"I didn't steal no hog," Daddy replied.

"I know you didn't," Mr. Bud said. "She don't have no hogs, but if she said you stole her hog, the law will lock you up."

"I need time," Daddy mumbled.

"You don't have a lot of time," Mr. Bud said. "She gave you three days."

"Three days! I can't find nothing in three days. I need more time."

"I asked around," Mr. Bud said, "and nobody in Marvis Town has anything empty. I figured you might find something downtown."

"I don't got no money for downtown," Daddy said. "How I'm gonna pay?"

"I'll take you downtown," Mr. Bud said, "and if we find something, I'll loan you the money. We'll work something out." Daddy left with Mr. Bud.

When they returned, I heard Daddy say, "Thank you. I'll pay you back." I was relieved. We were going to move, and Daddy wouldn't go to jail.

Mommy began packing that night, and we were ready to move by morning. There were things tied up in sheets, packed into pillowcases, and boxes all over the place.

"Get up!" Mommy demanded the next morning. "It's time to go." My feet had barely touched the floor when I heard the rickety old truck coming up the road. "Is everybody up?" Mommy called out.

"We're up!" brother responded.

We carried the small things out to the truck. Daddy loaded the truck, and off we went to our new home.

Summer came and went, and fall arrived. Mr. Bud came to get us to pick cotton. During the week, we stayed in the country in an old house owned by Mr. Bud's cousin. On Friday, we went home. Daddy worked in Columbia and came home on the weekends. I was grateful that Mrs. Madalyn had thrown us out. I liked living downtown. That was my first year in school, and Daddy brought me my first radio.

Mrs. Millie was a perky woman. I liked everything about her—her walk, her smile, and her kindness. She was always smiling. The day she came into the cotton field crying, I knew something was wrong. "Millie, what's wrong? What happened?" Mama asked.

"Oh, Anne," she gasped, "Coleman was found hanging in his cell. They say he hung himself. I know they hung him," she cried, "I just know it." Coleman was Aunt Kendra's brother. He was in jail for peeping in a white woman's window. Word was she was married.

Coleman was warned to stay away from her, but they continued to sneak out into the cotton field. She was supposed to meet him. When she didn't show up, he went to her house. He was caught and arrested as a peeping Tom. He was in jail awaiting trial. Mama and Mrs. Millie hugged each other. "I know they hung him," Mrs. Millie cried. "I just know it."

Aunt Kendra and Uncle Tim had also moved. They now lived in a place called Brusha Bay. It was on the other side of town, deep into the country. You had to drive for miles to get to them. When she found out, she burst into tears. "Why, God, why? Why couldn't he stay away from her?"

I had spent the first and second grade downtown. I was very happy during that time. Uncle Tim would pick us up on the weekend. We spent every Saturday and Sunday with them. Aunt Kendra would churn ice cream and bake a cake every time there was a birthday. Between her eight children and Mama's four, there were lots of birthdays.

One Saturday morning, Uncle Tim came to pick us up. He began the drive back to the country. Usually he and Mommy would be talking and laughing about something. Today they were silent. We drove the whole way without anyone saying a word. You could tell by the mood that something was wrong. We traveled down the dirt road deeper and deeper into the country. We finally reached the house. Me and Mama went inside, and brother followed Uncle Tim to the barn.

"Hey, Kendra," Mama called out as we entered the house.

"I'm in the kitchen," she said. Mama entered the kitchen, and I followed. Aunt Kendra was sitting at the table peeling potatoes. When we entered the room, she began crying.

"Oh, Kendra," Mama whispered, "let's pray everything will be all right.

"I know there's nothing we can do," Aunt Kendra sobbed. "Just like Coleman, Lance and Tarec were warned. Now the KKK is after them. Nobody has seen Tarec since yesterday, and Lance is scared to death. I'm so glad you came. I need someone to talk to."

"I need a drink," Mama whispered. They went into the bedroom. I went outside to find brother. "What does KKK mean?" I asked.
"Kill, kill, kill," he said.

On Monday, we went to Marvis Town to pick cotton. Me and Mommy left the cotton field and went to Mrs. Millie's house. She opened the door. She had a big grin on her face. "Come on in, Anne," she said. "I know you heard the bad news, but I have good news. They both escaped."

"How?" Mama asked, clearly puzzled. "I heard Tarec was picked up by a member of the KKK and nobody has seen or heard from him since."

"Ward was assigned to pick him up," Mrs. Millie explained. "On the way to the hanging site, Ward had Tarec hit him over the head with a tire iron. They threw the tire iron and the tire alongside the road. Tarec got into the trunk of the car. Ward drove to the hanging site, blood streaming down his face. He explained to the Klan that they had a flat tire. He said that Tarec changed the tire, and when he went to get back into the car, Tarec hit him with the iron. He told them he needed to go to the hospital. They went to look for Tarec. He then drove Tarec to a bus station in North Carolina, where he took a bus to Charlotte. Lance left this morning. They are both safe."

"Thank God!" Mama exclaimed. "Kendra will be happy to hear this news."

Mrs. Millie began to cry. "Why is you crying now?" Mommy asked

"I liked Tarec," she said, "but he was only a boy. I loved Lance. I'll never love anyone again as much as I loved him.

In 1949, we moved back to the country, to the farm of JC and Rue Marvis. Daddy took care of the whiskey stills. JC had a store at the crossroads, near Mr. Bud's house. The first three bails of cotton were out in the fields. Mommy got one, and JC got two. Red, JC's cousin, came to take us to the store to get the money. I could barely wait to get there. On the way, I could taste the candy. I knew just what I wanted: chocolate-covered peanut butter. What was a fifteen-minute drive seemed like hours. I kept peering over Red's shoulder as we traveled. As we crossed over the bridge, I could see the store located on the little spot at the crossroads, surrounded by cotton fields. As we entered the store, I could smell the food Mrs. Rue was cooking.

"Rue," Mommy called out.

"Come on back, Anne!" she shouted.

Mama went to the back of the store. I stayed out front, checking the candy counter. I had plenty of time. We had to wait until JC came in from the fields to pay Mama, and for Red to return from town.

After a while of chattering in the back of the store, Mrs. Rue and Mama came out laughing. They walked over to the side door. Mrs. Rue pointed to someone outside. "Look out there," she whispered. "That's mine. I raised him. His name is Billie. Hands off." They both returned to the back. I sneaked over to the side door and peeked out. There in the yard was a young colored boy raking leaves. Tarec, Lance, and Coleman came to mind. *Here we go again*, I thought to myself.

Red lived across the woods from us, and he sharecropped for JC. He had a large farm, and when Mama's cotton was out of the fields, we helped him. His wife and children worked in the fields, and he helped Daddy with the whiskey stills. Red and Daddy were both stealing whiskey. Red told JC that Daddy was the one stealing. JC became angry and threatened to stop furnishing him the supplies. Red and Daddy kept stealing the whiskey. JC stopped the supplies. Daddy and JC argued, and we moved off JC's place, farther out into the country.

We moved to the Roberts farm. Unis Roberts and his wife had one child, a boy. The house was large; the grape harbor made a nice play area on hot days, but I hated it. The only time we saw other children was in school, in the fields, or when the grapes ripened. The walk to the roadway where the teacher picked us up for school was long. The road was sandy, making the walk even harder. By the time we reached the crossroads, we were exhausted.

We were waiting for the teacher when the Roberts's son ran across the road and handed me a comic book. "Bring it back when you finish reading it," he said. He ran back across the road. When I brought the book back, I waved it in the air. He came running across the road, took the book, gave me another one, and ran back across the road. Each time I brought a book back, he gave me another one. The walk became easier now that I knew a book would be waiting.

One day when we were waiting for the teacher, he pressed his face against the window. I waved the book. He waved his hand and shook his head. "Uh-oh," I said to Louise, "he got caught." After that, he would come to the window in the morning and wave, but he never came out.

Without the books, I became bored, complaining to Mommy that I didn't have anything to do, anything to read. "Tell you what," she said. "I can give you something to do and something to read if you come work with me after school. All you have to do is sweep the yard for me and you can read Ellen's books, but only after you sweep the yard." I quickly agreed. Mama worked for a policeman named Andrew and his wife, Lucy. They had a daughter; her name was Ellen.

After school, I went to sweep the yard. I was amazed at the books Ellen had. Two shelves of books reached from ceiling to floor, and both shelves were full. Every chance I got, I went back. After sweeping the yard, I would go straight to the bookshelf. Then one day Ellen came home early and caught me reading. She became very angry. She snatched the book from me and called my mother. "Don't let her touch my books! She'd only tear them up." She sneered at me. "You can't read anyway. Leave my books alone."

On Saturday morning when Mama was getting ready for work, she shook me. "Lillie," she said, "you going with me?"

"Nope. She won't let me read her books."

"Oh, go with me," Mama said. "You can still read the books. Just don't take them off the shelf."

"If I can't take them off the shelf, how am I going to read?"

"There's more than one way to skin a cat," she replied. "Wait and see."

"Okay. I'll go."

Later that day, I finished sweeping the yard and ran inside. "I'm finished!" I called out.

"Pick out a book," Mama said, "but don't take it off the shelf. I'll be right there." I chose a book and waited for her.

She came into the room, and she had a piece of black cloth with her. I pointed to the book I wanted to read. She took the book from the shelf and stuck the cloth in its place. I smiled. Whenever I was there, Ellen would come check her books to see if they were out of place. When she finished, she would stick her tongue out at me. I would grin and stick my tongue out at her.

Ellen had entered a beauty contest and needed books on etiquette, and she got them from the library. Her mother came home late and didn't have time to take us home first, so we rode to town with them. I was excited because I had never been inside a library. Mrs. Lucy pulled up in front of the library.

"Can I get a book?" I asked Mama.

Ellen looked back at me and shook her head. "You can't get no books," she laughed. "They don't let niggers have books to tear up."

Her mother slapped her. "Watch your mouth," she muttered in embarrassment.

Ellen went into the library and came back with her books, crying once she got into the car. "You slapped me for nothing," she cried. By the time they dropped us off, Ellen had stopped crying. I got out of the car and waited for Mama to get out. Ellen tapped on the window. She was holding a book to the window, and it had a note stuck to it. "Stupid nigger," it read. I shook my head and walked away.

The next week, Ellen came home from school early. She had a friend with her. I was still sweeping the yard, and she started laughing. "See," she said to her friend, "I told you that's all niggers are good for. They can't do anything else."

I lifted the broom and started toward her. "Lillie," Mama called out, "come here."

I dropped the broom but sneered at her, "The day will come, you'll see, that I'm going to chop you up. Mark my words."

Mama never took me back to work with her. I really missed the books, but like Mama said, "Even reading is not worth the trouble you're going to get into."

The crops were out in the fields, and the Roberts came over on Friday night with pans of fish and hush puppies. "This is our thanks for helping us this year," Mr. Roberts said. He began chatting with Mama. His son got out of the car. I watched as he placed a bag under the car. He looked up at me and put his finger up to his mouth. He got back into the car. His father returned to the car, and they left.

I went to retrieve the bag. It was full of comic books, and a note was attached. It read, "Don't tell."

"I won't," I whispered as I hugged the books.

Mama came home upset from work one day. As soon as she got into the house, she started crying. She went into the kitchen, and I followed. "What's wrong?" I asked.

"It's nothing," she said. She took a glass and went into the bedroom. She reached under the bed, got the whiskey jar, poured some into the glass, took a drink, and sat on the bed.

"Now can you tell me what's wrong?" I asked.

"That little heifer," she sniffed, "caused me to lose my job."

"How?" I asked, knowing she was referring to Ellen.

She took another drink. "Remember the black box Lucy kept under her bed? Well, she put the change from her pocketbook in it every week. She had been doing it for years. Today she took it from under the bed, and it was nearly empty. She'd expected it to be full. She asked me if I had taken the money. I said no. She asked Ellen if she'd taken it, and she said no, so she assumed I had taken the money. She refused to believe me. She began to call me all kinds of names. I asked her to take me home, and she refused. 'You have to wait for my husband to come home,' she said. She kept calling him. I had to stay there and wait for him. All the while, she kept threatening me. I kept thinking he wouldn't believe me either. And if I was arrested, the courts wouldn't believe me either.

"When he got home, he was very angry but not at me—he was angry because she kept calling him. He asked me, 'Did you take the money?' I said no. He asked Ellen if she took the money, and she said no. He asked her if she was sure, and she said yes. 'Annie has worked here for years,' he said to Lucy, 'and nothing has been missing from the house.' He asked Ellen to come outside with him. When they returned, she was crying. 'Tell your mother what happened,' he said. She told her mother that she had taken the money to pay the children to vote for her because she wanted to win the beauty pageant."

"Then why don't you want to go back to work?" I asked.

She took another drink. "If you knew the things she said to and about me, you would understand." She refused to go back to work for Lucy, even though she pleaded with her.

JC bought some land within eyesight of the crossroads. It had a four-room house and a three-room clubhouse on it. He convinced Daddy to move into the four rooms and build him a store. We moved back to Marvis Town. Mama and Mrs. Rue were very happy about the deal. Daddy built the store near the highway, directly in front of the house. We loved being that close to the store. Mom and Mrs. Rue became inseparable. Billie plowed the fields for JC, and Mrs. Rue was pleased. She called him her Billie Dee.

A new family moved into the store at the crossroads. Ruddie was a former farmer and a known member of the KKK; his wife, Hanna, was a stay-at-home mom and Grand Dragon of her clan. They had two sons, Clay and Bret. One day brother came home after playing with the children. He was furious. He passed by me and went into the house. He got his shotgun and came out onto the porch to load it.

"You going hunting?" I asked.

"Nope." He jumped off the porch and went to the edge of the yard. He got some cans and placed them on bricks. "Come back and stand with me," he said. I did, and he handed me the gun, but I refused to take it. He shoved it into my hand. "I want you to shoot those cans down."

I shook my head no. "It'll knock me down."

"Not if you brace yourself." He smiled. "All you gotta do is brace yourself right." He positioned my feet and placed the butt of the gun to my shoulder. "Stay like that," he said. "Just aim and pull the trigger." The gun went off, and I fell to the ground, bursting into tears.

"Get up!" he yelled. "Get up and try it again." He picked the gun up and reloaded it.

"Daddy told you to stay away from those people," I said, "but you didn't listen." I got up and began to walk away. He grabbed my arm.

"Go ahead and run. Hide under the bed," he smirked. "When the KKK comes for you, I'm going to try and save you, but after they hang me, they're going to drag you out from under the bed and hang you too."

I took the gun, aimed at the cans, and pulled the trigger. The cans flew into the air. He grinned, took the gun, and walked away.

JC installed a jukebox and pinball machine in the store. The store became the hangout, especially on Friday and Saturday nights. We gathered at the store every weekend. At first, there was only five of us. My brother whom we called "Brother". He was fifteen years old, two years older than me. Louise, my younger sister was eleven years old and always acted as if she was older than me, and Dee, a nineteen year old that we met while working in the cotton field's of Mrs. Millie. Billie was there most of the time because he helped Mr. JC in the cotton fields and did chores for Mrs. Rue. Mrs. Millie had five children. Three girls and two boys. Aaron was the oldest son. He was twenty years old and drank a lot. He was the first of Mrs. Millie's sons to join the group. Aaron and Billie would sit in a corner of the store drinking white lighting until they fell asleep. One Friday me and mama was at Mrs. Millie's house. Brad said to me, "I know what Aaron do when he's at the store on Friday and Saturday nights, but what do y'all do?" "We play records and pinball." I said. "Oh! That can't be any fun," he said. I shrugged my shoulder and walked away. That Friday evening, Louise came home from the store crying. "Guess what?" she said, "Brad is at the store. He has a five dollar bill tied to a string. Every time someone comes into the store and sees it, they tries to pick it up. Brad pulls on the string and the money moves. I kept trying to pick it up because I thought the wind was moving it. He had everyone laughing at me." "Where is the money?" I asked. "in front of the ice cream box," she said. I got dresses and went to the store. Once inside, I went straight to the juke box. "Lillie!" Brad called out, "I'm buying ice cream for every one tonight. I turned form the juke box and starred at Brad. "Really?" I asked. "Yea." He said bowing his head. I walked over to the ice cream box and stepped on the money and picked it up. I popped the string and turned toward Brad. "Thanks." I said. Everyone began laughing. The next Friday, Brad came to the store. He had two more white teenagers with him. "Why did you bring them?" Louise asked. Brad rubbed his headed whispered to Louise, "I didn't want to be the only blonde headed, blue eyed person here." "Then dye your damn hair." Louise said. She had not forgiven Brad for playing the "Lost Money" trick on her. JC liked the income but did not like the whites and coloreds hanging out together. Mrs.

Rue loved it because Billie was there, and as she put it, "I can keep an eye on him." JC soon got a new jukebox and sold Daddy the old one. The gathering moved from the store into our house and the crowd grew larger. Every Friday we gathered the food and sodas for the party. The younger children also began to drink.

One Saturday morning when we were in the yard playing baseball, down the road came a Model T Ford. A lady was driving, and a young girl sat on the passenger side holding a baby. A small boy sat in the back, face glued to the window. They waved as they passed. They went into the clubhouse. A week later, they moved into the clubhouse. I later found out that the young girl's name was Jen. Jen was fifteen when she had the baby. She was now sixteen. The baby had the same name as his father. She never called him by his name. She called him" my bouncing baby boy".

She began sneaking out to the parties on Friday nights. Jen stayed close to me and Aaron because she could not get a date. Because she was taller than all of them, none of the guys in the group would ask her for a date. Her hair was stringy, and she was pale white. They called her plain Jen. As the night diminished, everyone would pair up and leave. By two o'clock, the only ones left were me, Jen, and Aaron. I tried to get Aaron to date her, but he refused because he had a crush on me. I thought that if they got together, they would leave earlier and I could lock the door before I went to sleep.

One Friday night I was so sleepy that I left the two of them up and went to bed. The next day when I went out to the tree to read, Jen was sitting on her steps. She picked the baby up and came running up the dirt road, excited. "Guess what! I kissed Aaron last night." She started giggling. "Oh God, Lillie, he is so nice. I love him already." Jen began sneaking out Friday and Saturday to be with Aaron. Her mother caught her coming home drunk and grounded her for a month.

I was outside under the tree reading when Jen came by on the way to the store one day. "Lillie!" she called out. I looked up to find her staring straight ahead.

"Hey, Jen," I said. "Still grounded?"

"Yeah," she mumbled. "I need to talk to you. Could you follow me to the store?"

I waited for a few minutes and hastily made my way to the store. I was going in the store as she was coming out. "Meet me under the shed," she whispered. I did. She began crying.

"What's wrong?" I asked.

"Mommy won't let me see Aaron," she blurted out. "She refused to meet him or let him come to the house when I asked." The tears were now streaming down her face.

I tried to reason with her. She cried and wouldn't listen.

"She said that anybody that hangs with colored people is up to no good." She sobbed.

"Jen," I said, "you're young. You will find someone else and fall in love."

"I don't want nobody else," she cried. "I love him. Will you tell him I love him?"

"I'll tell him," I promised.

Before her punishment was over, Jen began sneaking out again. She came by on Saturday morning and knocked on the door. I answered.

She laughed. "I got caught again, and Mommy didn't say anything. I think she's going to let me continue seeing Aaron."

"Is she going to let him visit you at home?"'

"I dunno," she said. "I'm scared to ask, but I'll be here on Friday and maybe on Saturday." She left with a big grin on her face.

A few days later, Daddy came home from work. "Annie," he said, "that woman that live back there bought a lot in Wallabout, and she wants me to build her a house on it, but she don't got no money. She wants me to build the house and she'll pay me later. I agreed to give her one day a week."

"That's why she didn't ground Jen," I whispered to brother. "She intends to move."

"Nobody's going to miss her."

Jen's mama picked Daddy up. The first day, he stayed all day. When he returned, he said he had laid the foundation. After that first day, he would return a few hours later with a chicken. After a few weeks, he became furious. "That damn woman won't buy enough material for a day's work," he grumbled. "She needs to get somebody who don't have a damn thing to do but waste time. I don't have time for that shit."

Daddy began hiding from her. Jen's mother would come by the house and plead with Mommy to ask Daddy to finish the house. Mama would beg him, but he refused to go back to Wallabout and finish the house. She continued to buy the materials every week. One day she came by and said, "Tell Shug I have all the materials he needs to put the building up."

Daddy was inside. He came out, and they talked for a few minutes. She left with a smile.

The next week, Daddy began building again. Each day, he went out and came back with a chicken. He would put the chicken in the pen and say to Mama, "Another day's work, another chicken."

Soon the house was up and the roof on, and Daddy came home with his chicken. "I'm not going back," he said to Mama. "She can finish herself. All she needs is sheetrock."

It was Friday night, and I had just popped the cap on a bottle of Pepsi when brother came into the kitchen. "Billie wants to see you," he said. He took the Pepsi. "Get you another one."

"Where is he?" I asked.

"He's on the porch." I walked out onto the porch to find Billie talking to Brad.

"You want me?" I said to Billie.

"Yeah. I need you to do me a favor."

"What kind of favor?" I asked.

"I need you to ride with me and Brad." He kept smiling. "You see, there's this new girl come from California, and she wants to go out with me. If you ride with us, it will look like you're with me and she's with Brad—you know, just in case we get stopped."

"Oh, no!" I exclaimed. "I am taking no part in you and Brad's schemes. Why can't you ride in the back and let her ride in the front with Brad?"

The car door slammed, and a cute young blond-headed girl got out of the car and walked over to the porch. She paused, one foot on the steps. "Hi, Lillie." She smiled. "I'm Briana. We won't be gone long. We just want to go get some beer and go someplace and talk. We'll bring you right back."

"I'm sorry. I can't go with you." I turned to go inside. Billie grabbed my arm and began to plead with me.

Aaron walked up to the porch. "She's not going nowhere with y'all," he said angrily.

"God dammit, Aaron," Brad yelled, "I thought you was staying home tonight!"

"I was until I overheard you and Billie plotting," he snapped. He looked up at me and pointed to Billie. "You should be ashamed. Why don't you tell her the truth—tell her that Brad intends to drop you and Briana off and drive off with her."

Brad jumped off the porch, got into the car, and slammed the door. Bre and Billie followed.

"Give me a ride home!" Aaron shouted as they pulled away.

"Walk, dammit!" Brad hollered back. The car roared off. Aaron walked away.

"Thank you!" I called out to him. He waved and kept going.

Billie kept sneaking into the cotton fields with Bre. Because his girlfriend was there, he would not bring her to the parties—moreover, Mrs. Rue might see her and wonder who the new girl was and who she was dating. Bre started coming to the parties looking for Billie, and he would hide if he saw her coming. Someone told her that he was hiding from her. This made her angry, and she began questioning some of the people in the group. Someone told her about Billie and

Mrs. Rue. They also told her about his girlfriend that frequented the parties.

One Friday night when she came to the party, Bre had been drinking. She became aggressive, insisting that someone find him. "I know that he's been hiding from me!" she said. She stormed out and slammed the door. Everyone cheered.

I woke up late Monday morning and went into the kitchen looking for something to drink. There was nothing in the fridge. I looked around the house until I found a nickel. I went to the store to get a pack of Kool-Aid. Just as I reached the side door, Mrs. Rue came out.

"I need your help," she cried, near tears. "That girl Billie was dating keeps calling here."

"What does she want?" I asked.

The phone rang. "Answer it," Mrs. Rue whispered. She pulled me inside, reached over the counter, picked up the phone, and handed it to me.

I answered it. "Hello. Marvis Grocery."

"Who is it?" JC called from the kitchen.

"It's for Lillie," Mrs. Rue responded. "She got it."

"Put that bitch on the phone!" Bre shouted. "She knows what I want."

"The bitch is already on the phone," I snapped quietly, "so what do you want?"

"You're not the bitch I want," she said. "You tell Rue that Billie is my man—and she is to stay away from him. I'm going to keep calling until I get JC. He'll put a stop to this shit."

"Tell you what," I whispered, "Billie is our man, and if you call here again, I will hunt you down like a hound dog. And when I finish with you, you will look like a tiger got hold of you. And when I say never call here again, I mean never." I slammed the phone down.

"God," I whispered to Mrs. Rue, "I hope she don't call back. I'll be in the yard if she does. Answer and say, 'Lillie is outside. Wait a minute—I'll get her.' And don't hang up."

Mrs. Rue moaned and shook her head. "But she calls all times of night. If she keeps calling, JC will know something is wrong." I went back and forth from the house and store until the store closed.

The next day, I waited until JC left and walked to the store. Mrs. Rue was in the kitchen. "Mrs. Rue," I called. She came out. "She call back?" I asked.

"No," she said, "but I couldn't sleep. I feared that the phone would ring and JC would answer it. I'm so sleepy that I'm afraid to sit down. If I do, I'll fall asleep."

After a Friday night party, Jen went home drunk. She could not get the door open. Her mother found her on the steps asleep the next morning. She was grounded again. Her mother made her sleep in the room with her. One day she came from the store drinking a Red Rock. I was sitting under the tree reading. She stopped and took a drink from the bottle. "How's Aaron doing?" she asked.

"Okay," I said.

"I need you to do me a favor. I need you to get him to meet me under the shed Friday night. I'm going to get pregnant so he'll marry me."

Astounded, I jumped to my feet. "Are you crazy?" I blurted out. "You have a baby already. That boy didn't marry you. What makes you think Aaron will?"

"He's different," she sighed. "He's a good person."

I was too stunned to say anything. I just shook my head.

"Don't forget."

When she walked away, I sat back down to read but couldn't concentrate. I kept thinking, *I can't let this happen to him.* She was right—he was a good person, too good to let anybody trick him into marriage. I had to tell him Jen's plan without making him think I was jealous. He may want to marry her, but not on her terms.

Friday night came and went, and I didn't tell him. Jen came by on Saturday morning. "Did you tell him?" she asked.

"He didn't come last night," I lied. "Brad said he didn't feel well—probably a cold. He may come tonight, and if he does, I'll tell him you want to see him, but don't wait under the shed until you're sure he's coming. Maybe he'll meet you next Friday night."

"Okay, but don't forget. I have to see him . . . I just have to."

I took a deep breath. "Jen," I said, "please be careful. These boys see girls as a game."

"Not Aaron. He's for real."

When she left, brother remarked, "Someone needs to talk some sense into that girl."

"She can't be helped," I sighed. "She loves Aaron; it's not a game to her."

On Sunday morning, she came up the road with the baby on her hip. I went out to meet her. "Did he come last night?" she asked.

"No," I said. "I don't know what happened to him; maybe he knows you can't go out."

She dropped her head and walked away. It hurt me to see her so unhappy, but I did not want to trick Aaron into marriage. The week passed, and I didn't see Jen all week, not even in the yard.

One day when I was sweeping the yard, Mrs. Rue[2] was in her backyard, waving for me to come over. I hurried over to the store. "Where's Anne?" she asked.

"She's asleep," I said.

"When she wakes up, tell her I want to see her."

Mrs. Rue had been crying. "Something's wrong," I said to myself, but I was afraid to ask. I walked back to the house, picked up the broom, and began to sweep. I was almost finished when I heard Mama call to me.

"Lillie, bring me some water."

[2]   Ms. Hanna lives in the old store at the cross road. Mrs. Rue lives In the new store that daddy built.

I took the water to her and told her that Mrs. Rue wanted to see her. "She's been crying," I said.

She took a few swallows of water, jumped out of bed, dressed, and left. I sat on the porch, waiting for her to return. Hours later, she came out the back door. I jumped off the porch and ran to meet her. "What happened?" I asked.

"Bre called again. She told Rue that she had alerted the Grand Dragon of the KKK about the niggers and whites that was sneaking off into the cotton fields at night, and that you had better watch out—the tiger might get caught by a rope.—and that she would keep calling until she reached JC."

As time passed, Mrs. Rue became more and more depressed. The fear of the KKK knowing about her and Billie, waiting for the phone call that never came, and the fear that JC would answer the phone if it did had her nervous and jittery. Her stomach had swollen, she was always nauseated, and she was tired all the time. She thought that it was from the sleepless nights. Word came that Bre had gone back to California, and Mrs. Rue became more relaxed.

Mrs. Rue's son came running up the dirt road crying. "Hurry," he shouted as he approached Mama. "Mommy's sick." Mama grabbed her scarf, tied it around her head, and ran out the door. I followed.

When we arrived at the store, Mrs. Rue was in the back, vomiting profusely. Tears streamed down her face. "You need to see a doctor," Mama said. "You're sick."

"No, I'm all right," she gasped. "Bre called." She looked at me and whispered, "Take him outside for me." I took her son out into the backyard.

JC came home while Mom was cleaning up. He insisted that Mrs. Rue see a doctor. Mama helped her get dressed. I could barely wait to ask Mama what Bre had said to upset Mrs. Rue. As soon as they left for the doctor, I asked her.

Mama took a deep breath. "She told Rue that she had told Hanna that her son was sleeping with the tiger—because she wanted her to die a horrible death. As for Rue, she wanted her to die in poverty. Rue became upset because Bre is in California and still calling. If she keeps calling, JC is bound to answer the phone."

The doctors said that Mrs. Rue had a tumor. She went to the hospital a few days later and had it removed; when she returned, she looked and felt better. However, the idea of JC finding out about Billie remained. The rumors of the KKK got worse, and Mrs. Rue was afraid that someone would tell JC.

Me and brother were watering the garden behind the store, and Mrs. Rue and Mama were chattering in the kitchen. We heard Mrs. Rue tell Mama she was a wreck and needed to get away.

"Where will you go?" Mama asked.

"JC found a place across the creek, but we don't have enough money to buy it." She paused and then said, "If the house you live in burned down, that would be enough money to buy that place, and it would get me out of this mess."

"Where would I live?" Mama asked.

"I dunno," Mrs. Rue said. "I'm just so scared and confused."

Me, Louise, and Lee were walking to Lee's house, and just as we reached the crossroads right in front of the store, a car drove up beside us and stopped. Brad stuck his head out the window. "You gals better stay off the highway." He grinned and pointed to me. "The KKK is out to get you."

I walked over to the car. Bret and Clay, Mrs. Hanna's sons, was in the car. Clay was sitting in the front passenger seat, and Bret and Aaron were in the back. "Y'all aren't making it better," I snapped, "stopping to tell us something we already know . . . in front of the store . . . and with Clay and Bret in the car."

"I told them not to stop," Aaron said. "It's better if y'all would travel the back dirt road."

"Better let us give y'all a ride," Brad said.

"No, thank you," I said.

Brad whispered, "The witch is out."

We turned toward the store. Hanna was standing against the store, a stick in her hand.

"Uh-uh," someone groaned, and the car lurched forward.

"Stay off the highway," Brad warned as the car sped away.

We refused to travel through the field roads. We thought they were more dangerous than the highways. Besides, that way was twice as long. We continued to travel the highway. Walking to Lee's house, when we reached the crossroads in front of the store, some rocks came rolling across the road. "Don't look up," I said to Louise and Lee. "Ignore them; they're trying to get our attention."

Louise laughed and reached down, picking up some rocks and throwing them back at them. "I'm going into the store," she said. "Y'all coming?"

"Not me," I said. "Don't go with her, Lee."

Louise finally convinced Lee to go with her. Louise went in first, and Lee followed. I waited outside for a minute and then decided I'd better go in and see what was going on. I went through the door and stopped. Bret was at one candy counter, talking to Louise, and Clay was standing at the other candy counter.

"Can I help you?" Clay asked.

"No," I said, "I don't got no money."

He reached under the counter and picked up a bar of candy. "You can have it," he said with a smile. I shook my head.

Hanna came from the back of the store and threw a glass bottle against the wall. It made a loud crashing sound. Louise looked at Hanna and burst into laughter. "Let's go," she snapped. "We don't want that rotten candy." They left the store, and I followed.

"I hope you know what you just did," I snapped. "You made things worse."

"Did you see that look she gave you? Boy, was she angry." I wanted to slap her.

A new girl came to town. She had been living in New York and was in Marvis Town visiting her parents and sister. She was the sister of one of the girls that frequented the parties. She was a beautiful person. Her **long silky** black hair hung down her back, and her olive skin seemed to glow. She looked at it she had just stepped off the cover of a magazine. The fellows said she was shaped like a Coke bottle. Mama said Daddy was head over heels in love with her. Her name was Candance ; Daddy called her Candy. Mr. JC had been flirting with her. She came to the parties, but spent most of the time at the store. Mr. JC called her that mulatta's gal.

I was under the tree reading when JC drove up. "Gal," he called out. I didn't answer. "Gal," he called again. I still didn't answer. "Lillie!" he shouted.

I looked up. "Yeah."

"Go inside and tell that gal to meet me at the hog pen," he said.

I put the book down, went inside, and gave her the message. JC drove off into the cotton field. Candance went out the back door to the hog pen. I peeked out the window. JC was coming up a row of cotton. He came and stood on the other side of the hog pen. They talked for a while. He left. She came back inside smiling.

"What did he want?" I asked.

"What do you think?" she giggled. "I'm going out with him tonight."

JC picked Daddy up that night, and they left.

The next morning, Mrs. Rue and Mama were in the kitchen peeling potatoes. I was in the backyard washing a cabbage and picking the worms off it. "Anne," Rue said, "did you know JC and Shug stayed out till early morning? When they returned, JC was drunk as a skunk. I was relieved. I think Bre is at it again. The phone rang twice when I answered it, and no one was on the line. JC went out right after and did not return all night."

"I don't think it was Bre," Mama said. "It's been months. Probably a wrong number."

"I hope so," Mrs. Rue said.

On Sunday, me and Louise went to visit our grandmother. She lived on the other side of the cotton field, at the bottom of the hill. When we reached the top of the hill, she came out of the house waving a broom.

"Don't come down here!" she screamed. "Gal, you can come if you're willing to take a whipping. I don't want that yellow one to ever step foot in my door again."

"Why, Grandma?" I called.

"You know why! Everybody knows you are sleeping with them cracker boys. Them Marvises have caused enough trouble; I refuse to let them cause me any more."

"What did the Marvises do to her?" Louise asked.

You know I said, "Those damn Marvin's kids." Louise laughed. "I'm going down there," I said to Louise, "I have to talk to her." "I'm not going," she said. "You go on and get your ass cut."

I slowly descended the hill. Just as I reached the edge of the yard, she dropped the house broom and picked up a yard broom. "Oh, shit," I uttered, "reckon she really is going to try and beat me. Grandma[3]," I said, "we're not sleeping with nobody. We're just friends."

"I don't care what you is!" she shouted. "Just stop seeing them, stop them from coming around." I was now only a few feet from her. "Come on and get your ass whipping." She smirked. I ran. She chased me with the broom, and round and round the chicken coop we went. When I realized she was tired, I ran for the hills.

When I reached the top of the hill where Louise was waiting, she was laughing so hard, she had to sit down. As we walked away, Grandma called, "You little heifers. Don't ever come back. Don't ever step foot in my house again. You're better off if the KKK hangs you."

"That's a loving grandma," I said to Louise.

---

[3] Every one called me Lillie, except Grandma and Mr. JC. Most of the time, I did not answer him when he called me Gal.

The party ended early the next Saturday night. I went to sleep, and when I woke, only Aaron remained. He was sitting by the heater, arms folded and head down. I realized he was cold. I placed a blanket around his shoulders and put some wood in the stove. He was still drunk, and his head wobbled as he tried to talk.

"Go back to sleep," I said, "and don't fall on the stove." I went back to bed, and when I awoke, it was nearly daylight. I opened the bedroom door and peeked out. The squeaking of the door woke Aaron.

"What time is it?" he asked.

"I dunno," I said. "You finished sleeping it off?"

"I think so."

"That's good," I said. "I have something to tell you."

"You're going to sleep with me?" He laughed.

"Stop playing, Aaron," I said. "Are you hungry?"

"Yeah."

I went into the kitchen. "There's some barbecue chicken left," I said.

"That's good," he said. "I'm hungry enough to eat a dead dog. I need something cold to drink too."

I brought the chicken out and placed it on the heater to warm. I handed him a Pepsi. He took a swallow and set it on the floor. He took a piece of chicken. After a few bites, he sat up in the chair. "You know, Lillie," he sighed between chews. "I'm not going out with Jen no more."

"Are you sure?" I asked. "Really sure?"

"Really sure," he said. "I don't like her."

"You might change your mind," I said.

"Oh, hell no," he exclaimed. "I'll never change your mind." He stood up and looked around. "Where's my coat?" he asked.

"You better wait until daylight," I said. "You have to pass a crossroads, and the witch will see you. She'll know where you're coming from."

"Naw, I'm going," he said.

"Then go through the field."

"Naw, I'm going down the highway." He shrugged his shoulders. "I'm not scared of her."

"Okay," I grumbled. "But when she realizes that it's you, she's going to get mad, and when she shoots you and drags you into the back of the store and says you tried to rob her, nothing is going to be done about it."

"I ain't scared of that witch," he said. He jumped off the porch and staggered off.

"Okay," I said, "I'm going to stay on the porch until you pass there, if I don't freeze to death before you reach the store, so at least I'll know what happened." I watched as he staggered down the dirt road and onto the highway. He walked down the highway until he passed the ditch, and then he stopped, looked back, waved, and disappeared into the cotton field. I breathed a sigh of relief and went inside. The fire had gone out, and it was cold. I jumped into bed and covered up, head and all.

Mama left early that morning with Mrs. Millie. Later in the day, I decided to visit Lee. I was afraid to go through the field roads or along the highway by myself. I took the shortcut through the cotton field to avoid Hanna. When I reached the highway, I was on the other side of the store near Mr. Bud's house. I could see Mrs. Millie's house. I kept walking and looking back. A car came up the hill, and I ran into Mr. Bud's yard. The car kept going. "I'm living like an escaped prisoner," I whispered.

I continued down the highway, and just as I reached Mrs. Millie's cotton field, I heard laughter. I saw Mama run into the cotton field, and Mr. Ward was chasing her. I ran into the cotton fields, and as I got closer, they disappeared. I ran faster as I got nearer, and then I heard more laughter. I stopped, bewildered. *How could she*, I thought, *knowing he was a member of the KKK?* Now I knew why she was able to walk into his store and leave with things without paying. The

Saturday before, she had walked by his store, picked up a heater, and kept walking. He pretended he didn't see her. I thought she had stolen the heater, but he knew. "Lillie, you're one stupid bitch," I whispered to myself.

I crawled out of the fields and into Mrs. Millie's yard. I sat on the front porch. Mama and Mr. Ward came out of the cotton field.

"You getting slower." She giggled. "I remember the time you would catch me before I got out the door."

"That was a long time ago," Mr. Ward said. "It was the night of the Joe Louis fight. God, how time's passed."

The back door slammed. I went and sat on the back steps. I was still sitting there when I heard Mr. Ward declare, "No, I will never leave the business to Brad. He'll just give it away. Within two months of my death, he'll be broke. Drinking, women, and business is a bad mixture. On the other hand, Aaron has a steady mind."

I got up and walked away. Everyone thought Brad, including Brad himself, would be the one to inherit the business. He was going to be very disappointed.

Jen's mother kept asking Daddy to finish the house. He promised that he would, but he hid when she came for him. Jen would walk by, wave, and keep going. She seemed depressed.

She was coming from the store, and I was going to the store one day. "Meet me under the shed," she mumbled as we passed. When I left the store, I went to the shed. Jen was sitting on a can, her head down, and she was crying.

"I want to see Aaron," she cried. "Mommy takes me to my aunt's in Wallabout when she leaves for work, and we're moving on Saturday. I'll never see him again. I get so angry that I want to run away."

"Jen, don't do that!" I exclaimed. "You have a baby. Tell Aaron where you're moving. Maybe he'll find a way to see you. Wallabout isn't that far. Please don't run away."

"Will you show him where I live?"

"Leave him a note," I said. "I'll give it to him."

"Okay," she sobbed. "Please give it to him."

A truck pulled up to the clubhouse on Saturday morning. Two men loaded the truck. When the truck left, Jen's mom followed. When they passed, Jen waved and dropped the envelope. I picked it up and stuck it in my book.

After party on Saturday night, Aaron woke from his drunken stupor. Everyone had left. The fires had died out. "Want me to start the fire before I leave?" he asked. "Well, I'm going to anyway. I have something to tell you."

"Really? What?"

He put some wood into the stove, poured some kerosene on it, and lit it. The fire went out. "Got any paper?" he asked. I went into the kitchen and got two brown paper bags. He rolled them up, stuck them under the wood, poured on some kerosene, and lit the paper. He pulled a chair nearer to the stove and sat down.

"Sit down," he said, pointing to a nearby chair. I took the chair and sat down. "Look," he said, "the KKK is really out to get you. It has something to do with Clay. I know it's a lie, but whatever Hanna wants, Hanna gets. You need to leave. It would really hurt me if something happened to you. Clay told me Hanna has cancer. It's not curable; she's going to die. I was thinking you could go up North. I'll go with you if you're scared. You can come back after she dies."

"You crazy," I said. "How we gonna live with no jobs and no money? We'll starve to death."

"I'll find a job," he said. "Millie will help us until I do. I don't have no future here. Ward is leaving the business to Brad; my heart is bad, so I can't do no strenuous work. In New York, I can get a job doing paperwork, what do I have here."

"More than you know," I said. "If you stop drinking so much, Mr. Ward will leave the business to you."

"How do you know?"

"I overheard him talking to Mrs. Millie and Mama," I said. "You can't tell anybody, because they would think I was eavesdropping, and I wasn't. Promise me you won't tell."

"I promise." He scratched his head and rubbed his eyes. "If you promise to leave, I promise to stop drinking."

"You also have to stop coming down here so often. And after I leave, you are not to come back at all." I smiled.

"Lillie, leave. I just need time. If you don't want me to come back, I won't be sad. But I heard your grandma don't want us together."

"She's just scared," I said. "She heard about the KKK." One of Brother's chores was to start the morning fire and wake the children up for school. That Monday morning, I could hear him stumbling around, and complaining. I was almost asleep when I heard him yelling.

"Wake up, wake up!" brother shouted. He ran from bed to bed. "The house is on fire!" He shoved us out the door and ran to the room where Mommy slept. "Get up!" he screamed. "The house is on fire!"

Harley was inside, and he ran out, pants in hand, hurrying into the woods. Brother burst into laughter.

A few minutes later, the house was ablaze. A soldier passing by saved the deep freezer—all else was lost. The Salvation Army gave Mama some beds and an old dresser. Mrs. Rue gave her some sheets and blankets. We moved into the clubhouse where Jen once lived. I wanted to ask Brother if he had intentionally started the fire to help Mrs. Rue get the money to move, but I was afraid to ask.

Mrs. Millie and Aaron came by. "I heard the KKK set the fire," Mrs. Millie said.

"I don't think so," Mama said. "Brother said that he spilled some kerosene on the floor. I think that may have started the fire."

"You promised to leave," Aaron whispered. "What happened?"

"I'm waiting for my aunt," I said. "She'll be coming through on her way to Florida. I'm going with her."

JC bought the land across the creek; it had three houses on it. JC and Mrs. Rue moved into the larger one. Mrs. Rue was happy. She changed her phone number.

"Just in case she finds you," Mama said, "answer the phone and pretend it's Candance calling for Shug." After they moved, JC didn't want Mrs. Rue and Mama to visit each other.

New people moved into the store, a cousin of JC's. The father, Victor, was a former prison guard, and his wife worked in the fields. Greta, his stepdaughter, had a baby. She came to the fields but did nothing. Greta began coming to the parties to meet Tom, the father of her baby. She found out he was dating Billie's girlfriend, and she began dating Billie.

I was helping Mama with the wash when Greta came down the dirt road carrying the baby on her hip. "Why does Billie keep dating these white girls?" I asked Mama. "Don't he realize we have enough trouble?"

"I dunno," she said, "but you can't live other people's lives."

The parties continued. No one but me seemed to think or care about the threats from the KKK. There were not any fights or quarrels among the group until our cousin Jeff began frequenting the parties. He began flirting with Greta. On a Saturday morning, she came down the dirt road with a big grin. When she reached the porch, she stopped and rested one foot on the steps.

"What's the big smile about?" I asked.

"Jeff," she giggled, "he's got it."

I jumped out of the chair. "Leave him alone," I said. "He's a fool, a real troublemaker. I'm telling you, don't sleep with him. You'll regret it."

"Okay," she muttered, walking away with her head down. She tried to keep it a secret, but I knew she continued to sneak into the cotton with him.

Friday night the party started early. Everyone was in and out of the kitchen cooking and eating. The photograph was blasting Elvis Presley's "Heartbreak Hotel." Brad came in and unplugged the machine. The crowd yelled at him to plug it back in. "Wait a minute," Brad said. "Just one minute. I have something to tell y'all. Elvis Presley said that the only thing a nigger can do for him is shine his shoes." Brad was the joker of the group. No one believed anything he said. A debate started as to whether Elvis said that or not.

Suddenly, there was a chilling scream from outdoors. Everyone ran outside. The scream came again from the cotton field. Greta came running from the field, and Jeff was right behind her, staggering and cursing.

"I'll kill that bitch!" he yelled.

Someone grabbed him and held him. Another demanded, "What the hell you doing, man?" They held him until we walked Greta home.

Saturday morning Greta came dragging down the dirt road as if she had lost her best friend. I went to meet her.

"I told you," I gasped. "I told you he was a fool. What did your father and mother say?"

"They're both mad as hell," she said, and she began to cry. "I told them I fell."

"They don't believe you," I said. "You have a black eye, a bruised face, and look at your arms. You can see the fingerprints. You'll hear more about this, you'll see."

Jeff was barred from the parts. He only came one time after that.

Me and Greta were walking to the store, and she was telling me how much she loved Billie. As we reached the side door, a car drove past. It stopped and backed up. A young man stuck his head out the window. "We're gonna get you, you nigger lover!" he hollered.

"Go to hell!" Greta shouted.

The side door was locked. We headed to the front, but I stopped and put my hands to my head. Greta opened the door and looked back. "Come on," she said. "What's wrong?"

"I was just wondering if you had heard the gossip about the KKK."

"Hell yeah," she said, but I'm not giving Billie up.

"What would you do if they caught you and him together?" I asked.

"Well," she sighed, "I'll have to say he raped me."

"That's lousy," I snapped. "After they hang him, we'll have to hang you."

We walked into the store in silence. She went into the back and slammed the door; I went to the ice cream box. A few minutes later, she came out and pretended to get ice cream. She bent over the box and whispered, "I'm sorry, but I'm scared too."

Daddy and Victor argued often. Word was they had been doing it since they were children. They would argue to the point of fighting, and the next day they would be laughing and talking as if nothing happened. After Jeff and Greta fought, he and Daddy still argued, but the arguments were more intense. They would go days without speaking.

We liked hanging out at the store because it had a pinball machine and they always got the latest records, but the attitudes were different now. Victor and Mrs. Tammie didn't want us to come into the store. Me, Louise, and Mrs. Tammie were in the cotton field. I had a portable radio, and a news brief came over the radio about the fight over school segregation. Mrs. Tammie blurted out, "I don't want my children in school with no niggers either." I was on my knees. She was standing. I looked up at her face, which was beet red. I was fighting mad. I stood up.

"All I need is for you to repeat that," I snapped, "and me and Louise will strangle you." She picked her sack up and walked away. As she left the field, I yelled at her, "You better not tell Mama."

When the word got out about Mrs. Tammie's statement, the colored people stopped patronizing the store and business got slow. Whenever me and brother were at the store and a car drove up to the gas tank, one of us would sneak up to the driver's side and whisper that there was water in the gas. The car would drive off. Victor soon realized what was happening, and he was furious. He was screaming at me and brother. "I don't want you niggers back in my store!" he shouted.

Someone heard him and told Daddy. He came running into the store with brother's shotgun. Me and brother were still in the store. He drew the shotgun on Mr. Victor. "What did you do to my young'uns!" he shouted.

"No, Daddy, no," I exclaimed. "It's our fault." Brother grabbed one hand, I grabbed the other, and we pulled him out of the store. Once outside, we told him how we had stopped people from buying gas.

"Leave Victor alone," he sighed as we walked away.

When Daddy walked off, brother whispered, "He didn't have no shells in that gun."

The parties got wilder. Everyone was sneaking into the fields with other people's boyfriends, girlfriends, husbands, or wives. I hated to see Friday night arrive. One party had ended, and I was asleep when I heard Mama screaming. I jumped up and ran outside. Daddy was dragging Mama across the yard. "You bitch, you gave Billie those shoes. Everybody is laughing at me because you're sleeping with the KKK. I'm not taking no more of this shit. I'm going to kill you."

I jumped off the porch, and my feet had barely touched the ground when Louise screamed. I turned around and saw brother standing on the porch, loading his shotgun. I ran back, jumped on the porch, and grabbed him. We fell off the porch, and the gun flew into the yard. I got up, grabbed the gun, and ran. I threw it into the field and ran back into the yard. Mama had gotten away from Daddy and hidden. He walked around looking under the house and cursing. When he couldn't find her, he went inside, got a jar of white lightning, and took a drink from the jar. He kept drinking from the jar until he fell asleep.

Mama came from under our bed. "Where's your daddy?" she whispered.

"Don't worry about him," I said. "He's out."

"We have to leave before he wakes up," she whispered. "Get the children. Millie will take us downtown."

We walked to Mrs. Millie's house, and she took us to town. "Y'all been fighting," she said with a smile. "Got caught."

"Yeah," Mama said, "I was too drunk to run."

We spent Saturday and Sunday with some friends of Mama's.

Monday morning when I woke, brother was standing beside the bed. "You hungry?" he asked?"

"No," I said. "I'm sleepy."

"I'm hungry. Go with me to get something to eat."

"You got money?" I asked.

"Nope," he said, "but I can get something to eat." He waited outside the room for me to get dressed. I peeked out the door. Mom's friends were lying on the floor naked. Brother ran over and grabbed my hand. "Close your eyes," he said. He led me out the door.

"What are you going to eat?" I asked.

"You'll see," he said. We walked until we reached a ditch. He pulled two nets from the ditch. They were full of crawfish. "Look at how many I caught!" he shouted.

"You're going to eat that?" I smirked.

He laughed. "Are you crazy? Come on."

I followed him down the bypass to a bait and tackle store. He gave the crawfish to the man, and he gave brother two dollars, which he stuffed into his pocket.

When we returned to the house, everyone was up, dressed and drinking again. "We're going to look for a place to live," Mama said. "Brother, you stay here. You're all muddy."

We walked and walked, looking for an empty house. I got tired of walking—besides, I didn't like what I saw as we walked. I wanted to go back to the country. "Let's go home," I said to Mama. "We'll go in first, and if he's still drunk, we'll hide. We'll be okay."

"You think so?"

"Yeah," I said. "You can get out at the store and stay. We'll come and get you."

"Okay," she said, "let's go home."

We went back to Mama's friends' house, got the children, and left. Mama got out at the store. We went on to the house. Everything had been removed from the house except the furniture. All the clothes, covers, food, curtains, everything . . . even Daddy. We ran out of the house and found Mommy coming down the dirt road.

"Your daddy's gone," she said. "Vince said he was going to Virginia—said he won't be back." Daddy never came back.

Harlen was now raking Mrs. Millie's yard. The gossip was that he was her new lover. Harley was married and dating Mama. Word got to Mrs. Millie that Harley was seen with Mama. He and Mama were walking to the store, and Mrs. Millie drove up, stopped the car, got out, and slapped Harley. He fell. Everyone from the store came out. A crowd gathered. People coming by stopped to see what had happened. The rumor spread among the crowd. A white woman had knocked a colored man down. Some were asking what happened.

When Mama heard someone say that she caught him with another woman, she hastily walked over to Harley, who was now standing. "Harley," she demanded, "why did you take Mrs. Millie's pocketbook? She ought to call the law."

"I'm sorry," Harley said. "I'll give it back. I'll give it back," he repeated.

"You'd better," Mrs. Millie stated. She got into the car and closed the door. "All my money better be in it, or I'll call the law on you.

Come on, Annie, you going to help me today." Mommy got into the car.

"Can I get a lift?" I asked.

"Sure," Mrs. Millie said. "Hop in." I got into the car, and off we drove.

Mama turned to her. "You're crazy," she laughed. "That is going to be the talk of the town." Now they were both laughing.

A few weeks later, Victor closed the store and moved his family into a house on JC's new place. Billie and his girlfriend moved into the other house. Billie continued to plow the fields for JC and keep Mrs. Rue pleased.

It was early in the day, and I thought if I was careful, I could get to Lee's house without anyone noticing me. I was a few feet away from the ditch when Mrs. Millie drove up and stopped. "You're who I'm looking for. I need your help."

"For what?" I asked.

"I have a hot date," she replied. "I need to look sexy but conservative, and I don't have anything to wear."

"Who's the lucky guy?" I asked.

"Ruddie," she said.

"He's the KKK; why him?" I shook my head.

"Please," she pleaded, "you don't understand. I love him. It don't mean I condone his behavior. Look at you. You're just beginning life. It's my last chance."

I saw the desperation in her eyes. "Okay," I whispered.

"Where are you going?" she asked.

"To Lee's house," I said.

"No, you're not," she said. "You're going back home and staying off the highway. Want me to drop you off?"

"No, I'm okay."

"Okay," she said. "See you tomorrow." I crossed the highway and headed back home.

The next day, Mrs. Millie picked me up, and we went to Chesterfield County. We stopped at a store, and she picked out a brown suit and beige blouse. I folded the suit and blouse and stuck it between my legs. As we walked to the counter, she whispered, "It's showing. When we get to the counter, I'll distract her so you can fix it." When we reached the counter, Mrs. Millie asked for a pair of stockings, and when the clerk reached down to get the stockings, I sneaked out the door and stood facing the window. I put my hands where the clerk could see them. She looked up at me and proceeded to wait on Mrs. Millie.

"Look at this," I said, pointing to the mannequin in the window when Mrs. Millie came out of the store.

She walked over to where I was standing. "Oh, that is pretty," she said.

"Walk behind me," I whispered. "I couldn't fix it; it's still showing." I walked away, and she followed.

Once inside the car, she started laughing. "I'm going to be sharp."

We left Chesterfield and went to Benson Town, where she parked the car. As we were walking to the drugstore, we completely forgot where we were. We were close together laughing because she had asked me to perm her hair. A group of young men came by and pushed me off the sidewalk.

"I still need you to perm my hair." She grinned.

I gasped. "You're crazy. I can't perm your hair."

"Yes, you can. I'll show you how."

She picked me up the next day to perm her hair. "Come on, Lillie," she said. "I have everything ready."

"Don't blame me when all your hair falls out." I giggled.

I did the perm according to her instructions. The smell was horrible, my eyes burned, and I kept sneezing. After I put the last rollers in, I patted her on the back. "Guess what," I said. "That stuff can kill you. There's got to be a better way. Please don't ask me to perm your hair again."

After drying and styling her hair, she stood in the mirror admiring her hair. "You did a good job," she said. She turned from the mirror, pointed her finger at me, and stated, "I need one more favor. I need you to babysit."

"Oh, no!" I blurted out. "I'm not staying in the house with them boys."

"They're going to the beach too," she said. "They're leaving before me."

"You sure?" I asked.

"Positive," she said. "They'll probably be at the beach before I leave home."

"Okay. I hope you're right."

When Mrs. Millie came to pick me up, she assured me that Brad and Aaron had already left for the beach. We put the children to bed, and she gave me some books and some covers for the sofa. She took one last look in the mirror. A horn sounded outside.

"That's him. See you tomorrow," she whispered as she left.

I got comfortable, watched TV, and read during the commercials. The phone rang, and I answered it. "Bitch!" the voice on the other end shouted. The phone disconnected. I thought it must have been Mrs. Hanna, but they wouldn't dare come to Mrs. Millie's house to get me. I lay on the sofa and drifted off to sleep.

The sound of the key in the door woke me. I sat up and waited to see who was coming in. It was Aaron. "I-I thought you were going to the beach," I stammered.

"I was on my way," he said. "Brad asked Clay to drop him off at the store; he wanted to ride with Bret. We met Bret later, and he said he wasn't going to the beach. Me and Clay figured that Brad had tricked us and was coming back here. So Clay brought me back home. Have you seen him?"

"He ain't been here," I said. "Maybe he went on to the beach with someone else."

"I don't think so," Aaron said. "He's probably someplace waiting for you to go to sleep. I have to lay down for a minute; I will not go to sleep."

"Oh God," I whispered. Aaron was drunk, and he'd be asleep before his head hit the pillow.

I put my shoes on. I tried to figure out an escape route. I could run into the field. He probably couldn't find me there, but I was afraid of snakes. If I ran down the dirt road, he would catch me before I got to the highway. I was still trying to figure out how to escape when I heard a *click, click* again. Aaron had left the door unlocked. Brad was already in the house. He had just locked both slide locks. I jumped off the sofa and ran right into him. He picked me up as if I were a rag doll and threw me across his shoulders. I began screaming, "Brad, put me down, put me down!"

"God dammit, Brad, put her down!" Aaron yelled. Brad dropped me. "What the hell are you doing home?" Aaron asked him. "I thought you went to the beach. You dirty son of a bitch. They tricked me. You were supposed to go to the beach with Bret. You knew he wasn't going to the beach."

"You saw Bret?" Brad asked.

"Yeah," Aaron said. "He told me he hadn't seen you."

"Okay," Brad said, "I'm going to bed." He entered the bedroom but left the door open. He could see me from the bedroom. After a few minutes, he called out, "Aaron, you asleep?" No answer. A few more minutes passed. "Aaron, are you asleep?" "No," Aaron said.

After a few more minutes, Aaron wanted some cold water. Brad went into the kitchen and came back past me with a glass of water. "I put some ice in it," he said to Aaron. "Drink all of it. It's nice and cold and it will wake you up."

There was a moment of silence, and then Aaron blurted out, "God dammit, Brad, you put whiskey in that water. You dirty bastard."

I panicked and stood up, but the floor creaked. I sat back down.

Slowly Brad called out, "Aaron, you asleep?" No answer.

I jumped off the sofa and ran. I didn't even know where I was running to. Brad was right behind me. I ran into the girls' bedroom and jumped into the bed between them. "Bell, wake up," I whispered.

"What's wrong?" she asked.

"You were moaning in your sleep," I said. "I thought you were having a nightmare. Go back to sleep, baby."

I looked up at the door. Brad was standing there with both arms stretched across the door. I picked the baby up and wrapped my arms around her. Brad left. I turned over and went to sleep. I knew I had found a safe haven.

I was making breakfast for the girls the next morning when Aaron came into the kitchen. "I'm sorry about last night," he said. "Are you all right?"

"I'm fine," I said. "I slept with the girls."

He took a deep breath. "I'm going back to bed," he mumbled. "I'm still drunk."

When Mrs. Millie came home, she swore she thought the boys had gone to the beach.

Mrs. Millie had another date with Ruddie and wanted me to babysit. I agreed. She laughed. "You're not scared no more?"

"No," I said. "I know how to avoid Brad. Aaron is okay."

She had barely left the house when the phone rang. I answered, "Marvis residence."

"Is this you, Lillie?" the voice asked.

"Yes, it is," I replied.

"Listen," the voice said, "you're not to walk the highway by yourself."

"Who is this?"

"Shut up and listen," the voice snapped. "When you go out, make sure you're with a crowd. Don't go nowhere with strangers. When you're home alone, stay inside." The phone went dead.

When Mrs. Millie returned, I told her about the call. "You need to leave here," she said. She dropped me off. As she drove away, she yelled, "Listen to whoever that was who called you!"

Mommy had sharecropped that year, and I wanted to help her get the cotton out of the field before my aunt came through on her way to Florida. We picked the last of the cotton on Saturday. My aunt arrived on Monday. We left that same day. When we got to Somerville, where my grandmother lived, I told my aunt that I was not going to Florida. I was staying with my grandparents. I had it all planned. I would go back to school. No more KKK worries. No more looking backward.

A few days later, another aunt registered me in school, and I was so happy. I was free to come and go without fear. I was in school for a few months. I fell asleep in class one day, and the teacher sent me to the principal's office. The man behind the desk looked up.

"Sit down," he demanded. "What's your name?"

"Lillie," I said.

He leaned forward, crossed his arms, and cleared his throat. "The teacher said you have stretch marks. Did you have a baby?"

"A baby? No, sir."

"Are you sure?" he asked curiously. "Stretch marks only come after you have a baby. We have to expel you from school until you can prove you did not have a baby. We can't have girls in school that are a bad influence on other children."

I was very disappointed. How could I possibly prove I didn't have a baby? To me, that seemed impossible. I didn't return to school, and no one asked why. It didn't seem to matter to anyone.

All my aunts and uncles had grown up and left home, except one. She was now married and had a child. My grandmother had been disabled by a stroke. My aunt stayed home to care for her. There was no one left to help on the farm. My grandparents moved from the country into town. Even though I wanted to go home, I was more content living in town.

I hated that part of the country. The only reason I had for staying in Somerville was to escape the KKK. I finally decided that I would rather hide from them at home than stay there. I wrote Mama, telling her I wanted to come home. She wrote back, telling me to stay a little while longer, saying she needed time to find somewhere else to move, that it was too dangerous for me there.

Mama moved and wrote that she was coming to get me. I was so happy. I ran to my aunt, saying, "Mama's coming on Sunday. I'm going home." My aunt was expecting. She pleaded with me to stay until she gave birth. I wrote Mama back and told her to wait awhile, that Auntie wanted me to stay until around Mother's Day. I wanted to stay because I wanted to name the baby. My aunt Susan came home before the baby came, and we fought over who would name the baby. She won. The baby came before Mother's Day. Mama came for me a week later.

Mama had moved a few miles from where we lived before. She was still in Marvis Town, but the house sat in a field off a dirt road. A row of trees lined the main highway, hiding the house. "Nobody will know you are home for a while," she said.

The cotton was ready, and we were in the field chopping it. I heard a snapping sound behind me, and I looked back. The foreman was behind me every time. I chopped; he would snap the whip. After about five minutes of chopping and hearing that whip snap, I grew furious. I began to chop down too many stalks of cotton. When he realized I was chopping down more cotton than I should have, he walked away.

After the cotton had been laid, me and mama went to visit Mrs. Millie, and mama was telling Mrs. Millie about the incident with me and the foreman. "I can't understand why he chose her to pick on," she said.

"Who's the foreman over there?" Mrs. Millie asked.

"Charles," Mama answered. "Charles West.

"Oh my God," said Mrs. Millie. "He's a member of the KKK. You got to move. Blanche has an empty house on her place. It's on the highway, not far from me. Ask her. She might let you move into it for a while."

A few days later, we moved into the place of Henry Marvis and his mother, Blanche. The only thing that divided the yard from the highway was a ditch. We were about a mile from the crossroads, on the only road that led from there to town. Mrs. Hanna was sure to find out who was living there.

During cotton-picking time, Mama always let us go home in the middle of the day when it was hot. We could come and go whenever we wanted, so long as we picked our quota for the day. It was the middle of the day, the sun was hot, and me and Louise had left the field and were on our way home.

As we were walking down the highway, Mrs. Blanche passed by. She stopped and backed up. "Where you gals going?" she asked.

"Home," Louise said.

"No, you're not," she remarked. "Turn your asses around and go back to the field."

"Go pick your own goddamn cotton!" Louise shouted.

"You brazen heifer!" Mrs. Blanche said. She sped off.

"She's angry," I said to Louise. "You shouldn't have said that."

"Old bat," Louise growled, "should mind her own business. She don't own nobody."